Love and Time

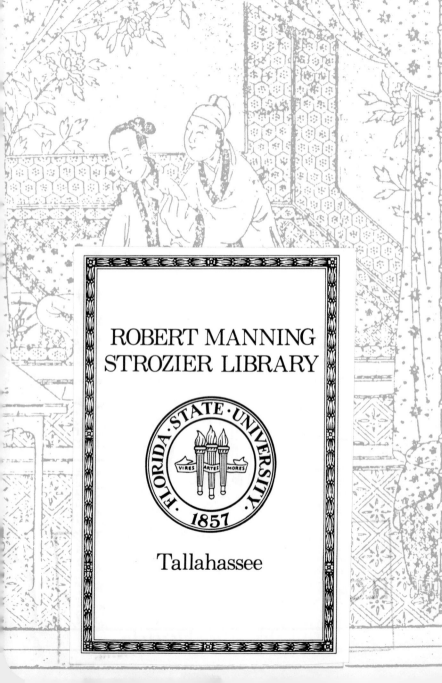

Love and Time

POEMS OF

OU-YANG HSIU

Edited & Translated

by J. P. Seaton

Copper Canyon Press

Port Townsend

Copyright © 1989 by J.P. Seaton
All rights reserved.

I S B N 1-55659-024-5
Library of Congress Catalog Card Number 89-61457

Some of these poems previously appeared in the
anthology *Sunflower Splendor*, and in *Human Voice*,
Hyperion, *The Literary Review*, and *The Sun*.

The publication of this book was supported by
a grant from the National Endowment for the Arts.

Copper Canyon Press is in residence with Centrum
at Fort Worden State Park.

Copper Canyon Press
Post Office Box 271
Port Townsend
Washington 98368

For the one I love,

KATHERINE PARADISO SEATON

Table of Contents

Note on the titles: *Tz'u* are conventionally arranged in collections under their "tune titles." These "tune titles," however, give nothing but an indication of required line lengths; they do not actually title the given lyric. The *tz'u* in this collection are titled by first line, according to English convention. The quatrains are titled as in the original.

Introduction

Vital, honest, forthright, warm, and witty: these words appear in nearly every biographical study of Ou-yang Hsiu (1007–1072) and in nearly every critical study of his poetry. So close was the art to the man. He was an idealist; he was a pragmatist; pioneering epigraphist and major historian; lover of women, lover of wine. He was friend to many men, patron to the finest literary minds of his time; masterful and innovative poet, and founder of a school of prose writing (called *ku wen*, or ancient writing) which was to remain the dominant form of expression from his own eleventh into the present century. All of these things and more, Ou-yang Hsiu was, of all the greats, closer than any to the Western stereotype of the Chinese poet as scholar-official-literatus. Certainly each of those categories held a special appeal to Ou-yang Hsiu; none, on the other hand, could hold the man himself. He was an individual in a society where individuality was particularly hard won, and a man of many finely cut facets.

Born in 1007 in the Western frontier of Sung Dynasty China, Ou-yang lost his father when he was four. Poverty and the lack of parental instruction weighed heavily against the possibility of a first rate classical education for the young Ou-yang, but the rise of printing in early Sung made the Confucian Classics widely available at an affordable price for the first time in

Chinese history, and Ou-yang, like many others in his time, was largely self educated. The individualistic approach to the interpretation of the Classics that he took, and that he later fostered among a major faction of the Sung scholarly and literary elite, can certainly be seen as a by-product of his lack of a conventional education. That his unconventional education did not hamper his rapid development as either a scholar or a literatus offers an indication of the energy and the genius of the man himself; it also clearly shows the lively and untrammeled nature of the political and intellectual world of the early Sung. Great changes were afoot in the China of the eleventh century, and Ou-yang Hsiu was to play an important role in many of them. He began his rise to fame and influence, at the age of twenty-three, by achieving the coveted *chin shih* degree, the highest honor available through the Imperial Civil Service Examination System, and the guarantee of an opportunity for employment in the Imperial bureaucracy. He was already recognized as a rising poet.

Ou-yang's political career was long and eventful, involving him as a leader of the progressive faction of the Minor Reform (1043–44) in his youth, and of the conservative faction in the first years of the Major Reforms (1069–85) late in his life. Whether it was pragmatic, as in the period of the Minor Reforms, or more idealistic (or at least more ideological) in the later period, Ou-yang's position was consistently and clearly a Confucian ethical position. And though the period produced savage political infighting (Ou-yang himself was twice accused of incest, the politics of personal morality being nothing new to the Chinese), a reputation for personal honesty and political ethics is a major feature of the picture of the man which has come down to us through a thousand years of Chinese history. In his personal life he made for himself quite another sort of name. In his early years, a number of his friends cautioned him for his frequent carousing in the courtesan quarters. In later life he bestowed upon himself the title of "The Old Drunkard."

While the philosophical trend of his time turned toward the metaphysical vein that was to produce the Neo-Confucianism of Chu Hsi in the next century after his death, Ou-yang's personal philosophy, hard won in his youth by the private study of the classics and tempered in the practical political struggles of a long and eventful life, remained consistent with the rational, skeptical, and pragmatic ethical social commitment of Confucius and Mencius. In government, Ou-yang valued action over words, just as he valued individual expression above the constrained formality and over-refinement of the dominant poetic forms of his youth.

A look at Ou-yang's position in Chinese literary history gives a clear indication of his individuality and his power as a creator. Like most of his contemporaries he wrote in two forms: the *shih,* which actually included at least four very well defined types of poetry, and the *tz'u,* a species of song lyric that Ou-yang almost single-handedly raised from the status of a popular plaything to the vehicle for the best poetry of the Sung period. In the realm of the more traditional *shih,* Ou-yang was also an innovator, or at least a renovator, actively opposing the preeminence of the effete Hsi-k'un style which had been in vogue for nearly two hundred years. The Hsi-k'un poets, products of the dangerous times of the late T'ang, limited themselves to innocuous and conventional topics, larded their verses with allusions of the most arcane sort, and combined intricately parallel grammatical constructions with elaborate figures to make a poetry that is hard not to call decadent. Ou-yang's *shih* poems confront the foppish Hsi-k'un with just the sort of self-assured directness that one might expect from a self-taught genius. They have a clear and simple diction that marks them at first glance as something quite other than frilly Hsi-k'un verse.

The quatrains that end the selection of poems translated here fall far short of presenting the full range of Ou-yang's *shih* in terms of thematic concerns or technical accomplishments, but they do offer, nonetheless, good examples of his precise word choice and direct self-expression. They are very much in the tradition of the High T'ang, expressing a highly individual vision of the world in a sharp and unpretentious manner. Nor do they lack depth. Certainly the vision of "Lang-yeh Creek" is as beautifully mystical, as much a vision of ultimate reality *embodied* in simple phenomena as any of the justly famous poems of the T'ang master Wang Wei.

In his *shih* poetry as a whole, as in other areas of his life, Ou-yang is primarily a rationalist and a pragmatist, guided by a strong sense of Confucian ethics. Social themes are not absent from his *shih*. But here Ou-yang *glories* in what to others may seem mundane; he does not merely dwell in it. The "source" (and the double meaning here is the same as in the English) is unknowable, certainly, except in its manifestation in the moment. The miracle of the flowers is the miracle of the stream. The door to all mysteries, as the first poem in the Taoist Classic

Tao Te Ching says, is precisely in the indivisible pairing of the source and the flower.

Ou-yang brought the strengths of his *shih* poetry to bear on the creation of poetry in the *tz'u* form. The majority of the poems translated in this volume are *tz'u*, a late T'ang innovation characterized by lines of uneven length. The form first flourished among professional female entertainers, where it continued to have a creative life even after it was appropriated as a plaything of the literary elite (who undoubtedly learned it in the high class brothels and geisha houses of their time). *Tz'u* were written (or "filled in" as the Chinese say) to conform to the line pattern of one or another "song" chosen from a group of over five hundred possible titles. Once the tune was chosen, *tz'u* form required conforming to a set pattern of line lengths. For instance, a *tz'u* written to the tune of "The Butterfly Loves Flowers" required two stanzas, each with lines of seven, four, five, seven, and seven syllables (or characters, since each character is mono-syllabic) with rhymes on all but the four character line, while one written to the tune of "Southern Boy" had lines of four, seven, seven, two, and seven syllables, with rhyme absent only from the second seven. In the most formal version it required prescribed tonal variations within the lines. While "filling in" *tz'u* could be a demanding discipline, it is also possible to create a *tz'u* by writing in more or less free verse, then cutting and pasting to fit the available form most similar to the verse. (The poems of Chairman Mao, which are mostly *tz'u*, were probably created in this manner.) From the beginning of its popularity in the T'ang, the *tz'u* was something less than a totally "respectable" form because of its origin outside the elite, and because it was used, both by its original creators and by their elite clientele, as a vehicle for erotic description. The manner of Ou-yang Hsiu's use of the form is another mark of his originality and influence. Critics generally agree that it was his use of the form in the West Lake cycle included here (p. 20), a group that extends the thematic range of the form well beyond its previous limits, which popularized the *tz'u* as a vehicle for personal lyrical expression. Poets who wrote *tz'u* before Ou-yang clearly regarded their *tz'u* poems as playthings, as something less than *real* poetry. Ou-yang replaced the conventional, flimsy, romantic lyric (in the hands of the elite versifiers sometimes faintly or faintingly erotic, and usually delivered in a feminine persona) with a direct, warm sensuality, usually delivered in his own voice; and he added themes of friendship and Taoistic acceptance. The robust warmth of the poet's personality revivified the form and his contemporaries were not slow to recognize the fact with praise. In the works of Ou-yang Hsiu's most famous protege, Su Shih, (Su Tung-p'o, 1037– 1101), the *tz'u* takes its place as an equal partner with the *shih,* and in the latter half of the Sung, *tz'u* poetry provides the major vehicle for poets as diverse in approach as the fiercely female Li Ch'ing-chao (1084?– c.1151), acknowledged as China's greatest woman poet; and the equally fierce poet-general, Hsin Ch'i-chi (1140–1207).

For the last hundred years or so Chinese as well as many Western critics have celebrated the *tz'u* as the "flower" of Sung poetry, much as the regulated *shih* of the T'ang is portrayed as the flower of the Golden Age. Recently several scholars, following the lead of the great Japanese Sinologist Yoshikawa Kojiro, have argued that the various forms of *shih* poetry actually remained the primary vehicle for the expression of high themes and major emotions. Perhaps the crux of the argument lies in the definition of high and of major. Certainly the *shih* forms continued to be used for the engagement of social, political, and orthodox Confucian philosophical issues, while the *tz'u* came increasingly to be used for the more universal themes of lyric poetry: the passing of youth, the coming of old age and death, the imperfections of human life. In Ou-yang Hsiu's *tz'u* (and increasingly in the works of those who followed along his way) there exists a subtly discernible personal mixture of the three great philosophies of his time, the Confucian, the Taoist, and the Buddhist. Though he was a vocal opponent of politicized Buddhism (and of its leader, his one-time protege Wang An-shih), most of the *tz'u* and quatrains offered here state at least the first two of the Four Noble Truths of Buddhism: Life is (essentially) suffering; suffering is caused by craving. If Ou-yang appears to depart from the Buddhist line at this point, occasionally counseling the twisting, sometimes twofold path of wine rather than the Buddha's Eightfold Path, his solution coincides, perhaps ironically, with that of the Ch'an Buddhists. Nirvana is samsara for Ou-yang Hsiu, and samsara, nirvana. One does the best one can, in politics, or in love. One respects life, in oneself and in others. One loves, and grows old. There is nothing to fear, and nothing to care for, but love and time.

•   •   •

For the reader whose interest in the poet and his period has been piqued by this short introduction I can happily recommend two excellent, short bio-critical studies in English. The first, *Ou-yang Hsiu, An Eleventh Century Neo-Confucianist,* by James T. C. Liu (Stanford, 1967), certainly sparked and fed my interest in Ou-yang and his poetry over twenty years ago. The second, *The Literary Works of Ou-yang Hsiu, (1007–72)* by Richard C. Egan (Cambridge University Press, 1984) offers many new insights and some very fine translations.

•   •   •

The poems offered here were translated in odd moments and longer spurts from 1967 to the present. Irving Y. C. Lo was an important instigator of my efforts. Charles Hartman and Eugene Eoyang may have forgotten their contributions. Carolyn Kizer and Sam Hamill have changed my thinking (and my words) more than once. Thanks to you all. I claim the credit for all errors, be they caused by ignorance or by stubborn and misguided pride. I love the poems, and I hope it shows.

J. P. SEATON

Love and Time

By the Lake the Bright Red Bridge

By the lake the bright red bridge
sounds with the wheels of painted carriages.
The surge of spring is in the stream
and spring's clouds, like desire, rise,
yet the water's green as glass and polished clean,
a mirror clear of anything of earth's.
Drunk, and on the road, I am
bound in floating threads of spring.
Blossom hidden, a bird calls the traveler back.
The sun slants away as I return.
What's to be done with spring?

First Moon, the Handle of the Dipper
Turns toward Spring

First moon, the handle of the Dipper turns toward spring.
With golden blades they scissor flower pennants for the fete,
And, feasting in high halls, the young enjoy themselves.
See the meaning in the willow's sway: winds from the east,
Spring's on its way.

Fourteenth, the moon still not quite full.
Before the hall there, look, the first red lantern tries the night.
The ice breaks up, fine strands of water green the pool.
Fish will be playing soon.
In the courtyard grove, already flower weather.

Snow Clouds are Suddenly
The Blooming Cumulus of Spring

Snow clouds are suddenly the blooming cumulus of spring.
I come aware the year's a flower fit to lead the eye
to northern branches where the plum buds brave the chill
       to open,
or southern shore where ripples wrinkle green as wine.
The fragrant grasses wait in turn to bloom.
I can't endure these feelings; no place to find relief.
Before my cup, I'll scheme a hundred schemes to bring
       spring on,
and won't, though spring wounds deep, sing sadly.

After the Swallow and the Swan, the Spring Goes

After the swallow and the swan, the spring goes.
I reckon carefully the million wafting silks, this floating life,
come, like spring dreams, to last how long?
Gone, like morning clouds, beyond searching.
I heard the lute, untied my sash among mild spirits,
yet though my grasping tore their silken robes,
I could not keep them:
                              (who can hold the spring?)
Don't stay the only sober one:
There must be many
                    sodden drunk
among the flowers.

You Cannot Hold It...

You cannot hold it...
Pretty girls grow old
and indolent; there is an end to spring.
When breeze is warm and moon so fine,
if you can manage yellow gold, buy smiles.
Nurture the tender blossoms there, don't wait.
No flowers to be plucked
from empty bough.

West Lake's Good: Ten Verses

I

A little boat with stubby oars, and West Lake's good.
Green water winds a vagrant wake,
Fragrant grasses stretch the dike.
Strange, the small song of the reed-pipe follows.

Windless, the water's face is shimmering smooth.
Unnoticed, boats glide by.
The slightest motion, and ripples flow.
Startled, sand birds thrash up the bank.

II

Deep spring, rain past, yet West Lake's good.
The grasses vie in elegance,
a butterfly confusion, clamour of bees.
Clear day, buds about to burst to flames of sun.

Far off, a painted barge disturbs the lilies,
or maybe it's a band of sprites reflected in the waves.
Tossed on broad waters, riding the wind high up,
music – flute and strings.

III

A painted skiff with a load of wine, and West Lake's good.
Urgent pipes and quarrelsome strings,
a jade cup demands attendance.
Afloat on peaceful seas,
I'll accept the post
of drunken sleeper.

Clouds float beneath the moving boat.
Empty waters: pure and fresh.
Look up, look down; stay, or go on.
There's another heaven
                    in this lake.

IV

Flocks of blossoms gone, yet West Lake's good.
Shattered, scattered residue of red
as willow-down comes misting down.
The willow hangs across the wind all day.

The pipe song wanders off, the traveler goes,
and spring feels suddenly empty.
I let the gauze curtain fall.
Fine rain, and mated swallows coming home.

V

You can't explain its joys, yet West Lake's good;
its beauties, timeless.

Carriages rush by
as I sit lusting for the flowers,
drunk beside a fine jade cup.

No one sees me where I idle by the rail.

Fragrant grasses in dying glare.

Above far waters, secreted in mist,

Isle of Immortals Egret, flying, single, white.

VI

Festival morning! West Lake's good!
Everything's woven in blossoms.
Why speak?
Red wheels of noble carriages among green willows.

The ramblers return together in the sunset,
the drunk and the sober, trailing bright petals of chatter.
The winding road, the steep embankment,
all the way to the city wall,
everything flowers.

VII

When the lotus opens, West Lake's good.
Just come with wine,
no need for pageantry,
or serried ranks of carriages in train.

The painted skiff slips deep among the flowers.
Fragrance drifts round the golden cup,
misting rain misting.
Go back, drunk in a phrase from the reedpipe.

VIII

Sky's face, the color of water, West Lake's good.
Cloud beasts changing, springing fresh,
terns and egrets napping.
I do as I've done, and I will myself music.

Clear breeze, the moon white, a night nearly perfect.
A patch of good earth,
and who'd covet honors.
In a boat, any man's a sage.

IX

Storm tatters in the dying glare, and West Lake's good.
Flowers on the bank, duckweed on the sand,
ten acres gentling waves.
By the wild shore, alone, the skiff hangs
above the water.

Southwest, a risen crescent drifts on scattering clouds.
Here, by the railing, a coolness is born,
the pure fragrance of lotus.
From the face of the water, a breeze,
to sober a man.

X

A whole life of saying, West Lake's good!
Now the people press about the carriage.
Wealth and honor? Floating clouds.
Look up, look down; the rushing years:
two decades.

I come back, old white head, ancient crane.
The people of the city and the suburbs,
all strange; all new.
Who'd recognize the old coot, their master, on another day.

They Made Ready on the Stage

They made ready on the stage,
composing sleeves and gowns,
and then their songs wound
to carved beams, to startle dusty darkness.
Soft and smooth and clean and round,
as pearl and pearl upon a single thread.
Cherry lips and white jade teeth,
Spirits of the sky above, sing of the hearts below.
Hold these fleet clouds!
This drunken watcher's soul's beguiled.

Here Clear Freshet Breasts the Stream's Green Waves

Here clear freshet breasts the stream's green waves.
New pavilion; mountains face from all four sides.
Bright moon on the bamboo's craggy tips...
Look up, or look down, the wheel of the moon's in the pool's
    ripples too.

The more because we waited for high autumn's lively air...
Scent of chrysanthemum, new vintage opened;
Fine wine, good friends, these are the greatest gifts.
Here beauties sing, and strange the sound,
deep among the mountains.

The Sound of Beating Oars Wafts in among the Flowers

The sound of beating oars wafts in among the flowers.
This shy, gentle girl comes in search of me,
brings lotus leaves to sip from . . .
Our skiff rocks among the lilies,
little red waves in the wine.

Her way, wine fragrance, pure as fine vintage.
The flower's face flushed, the drunkard's pink; we two facing.

Drunk, we rested in deep shade; we napped awhile,
and woke to find
                    the boat stuck on a sandbar.

The Lamp-wick's Ashes,
Blossoms Droop, the Moon like Frost

The lamp-wick's ashes, blossoms droop, the moon like frost,
now light of sun and moon together through the screen.
Almost too drunk, she has a fragrance of her own.
Two hands, the dancing done, grasp blue-green sleeve.
In the sound of the song we'll drain the cup again.
Don't turn your pretty face away,
You'll break my heart.

Sound As the Sandalwood Stops Are Set

Sound, as the sandalwood stops are set,
and then thrum of golden strings.
Dew dampens the moon on Hsun-yang stream.
For whom does the merchant's wife grieve?
One crooked file of travelers,
departing from their haven of the night.

In painted hall among the flowers in moonlight,
the songs of parting sounded.
"Red Petals" long drawn out, and lingering in the air;
there in the dark, yearning, we prayed,
May the song of those strings never end.

The Pear Leaves Redden, Cicada's Song Is Done

The pear leaves redden, cicada's song is done.
Wind high up in the River of Heaven,
flute sounds: cold and cutting.
A chill on the mat, the water-clock dripping.
Who taught the swallows to make so light of parting?

At the edge of the grass the insects moan,
as autumn's frosts congeal.
Stale wine: awakening,
I can't remember when you left.
How much of what I really feel is left unsaid?
Night after night moon dawns
upon my pearl embroidered screen.

Faint Thunder Drifts beneath the Willow

Faint thunder drifts...

            beneath the willow,

rain upon the pool.

The sound of rain,

and rain again from lotus leaves.

The western eaves of this small place

cut through the rainbow.

I leaned on the rail and waited

for the moon to bloom.

A swallow flew and perched

            to peer in at the ridgepole.

The moon, jade hook,

hung from the curtain rod.

No waves on water,

still waves, the wrinkles of the coverlet.

Behind the crystal screen, two pillows:

on one, a hairpin fell.

The Pool is Full of Autumn Sky,
Rippled by Gentle Breezes

The pool is full of autumn sky, rippled by gentle breezes.
Strange misty skiff mounts on that sky,
and with the dew I pluck the lotus,
gift of autumn; on my heart,
the very flower marked with tears.

When you snap the lotus stalk,
the threads hang on.
Break the blossom off, stretch out the threads:
draw out your heart.
As I sail home, I'll turn my glance
from lotus flowered margin of the waves:
from the shore, someone gazes.

She Plucked Lotus

She plucked lotus
by the bank of an autumn stream.
Beneath the gauze of her narrow sleeve,
two golden bracelets at her wrist
reflected flowers as she picked,
and then reflected her face.

My heart raced with the spring...

Egrets at the stream's mouth; late; wind and waves
mist deep, haze rising.
I cannot see her anymore.
Her song's in the depths of darkness, her boat far away:
The sorrow of the parting drawn
clear to the other shore.

Light Wind's in the Curtain,
A Pair of Swallows Murmur

Light wind's in the curtain, a pair of swallows murmur.
I'm finally sobering at noon,
as the down of willow flowers
comes falling, floating, down.
The whole spring without you:
red petals all cover the court's green moss.

I lean, high in the vermillion hall.
Light rain and rolling clouds
beat down the watcher's face.
No need to pipe again the pain of parting:
I've no heart left to break.

Half-Drawn, the Screen of Pearls

Half-drawn, the screen of pearls,
incense obscures the mirror.
East wind in the second moon

               brings news of willows greening.
Does she sit beside her moon-guitar

             thinking of me?
I sit before the parrot cup,
don't dare to ask the wine.

She's gone like a frightened swan: the pain of parting grows.
The red sun lengthens, I only add to the pain with wine.
No way to know with whom my heart lies now:
Eyes pearl with tears.
Words fail.

After Parting,
No Knowing Now How Far You've Gone

After parting, no knowing now how far you've gone...
I gaze into the cold, at so much pain.
Longer going, longer gone; I long for a letter.
The waters broad, the fish, those fabled messengers, fled deep.
Where then to ask for news of you?
Night deep, wind in bamboo beats rhymes to autumn.
The sound of each and every leaf is pain,
and so I sigh and pull my lonely pillow to me
to search for you in dream,
but dreams won't come:

the wick's burned to ashes.

Deep, Deep in the Shade of the Court

Deep, deep in the shade of the court,
the oriole flutters and sings.
Sun warms, the mist warm; spring breathes heavily again.
Green eyes, the willow leaves now turn toward whom?
Across the distance, fragrant grass spreads out,
brooding, vacant, restlessly moving.

Wordless, she suffers, wounded that he'd go.
A shudder of love for him, and no way to show it.
She worries and worries, and finds her heart unchanged:
over and over when she sleeps
the butterfly's imprisoned in her dreams.

The High Hall Faces Dawn

The high hall faces dawn.

A pale moon droops beneath the clouds, fair weather.

Faint breeze in the kingfisher curtain,

then the strains of "Yielding Turning" yield and turn,

"Cool Shores" begins abruptly.

A fragrance is borne in her dancing sleeve.

Beauty she is, slim loins heaven given.

Perspiration, makeup, mix,

but when the wine is gone, a chill...

No one waits to carry her away.

In Pairs the Petrels Come Again
To Find the Painted Beams

In pairs the petrels come again to find the painted beams.
No breeze in the curtains,
but flower shadows restlessly moving.
Half drunk, slow with spring's languor, her
glossy hair piled, clouds upon the pillow.
A pair of golden hairpins lie
on her blue-green coverlet.

Remembering another spring,
two people there together,
the golden oriole at play among the flowers,
surprised by slanting sun, she rises
from her dreams of him.

Beneath the Leaves' Green, Green Apricots Hang

Beneath the leaves' green, green apricots hang,
and branches bare themselves to fill the air
with flying willow silk.
The sun is high, yet court so deep
the orioles of evening cry.
She bears her pain, nowhere to go.
His breezy elegance
now seems so frivolous.
Cut off, no news, who'd say when he'd return?

Winter's Snow Begins to Melt

Winter's snow begins to melt,
the plum to spread its petals.
Plum's white and snow's, a harmony.
The magpie sings to blossoms.
When I woke, the waning light
confused my drunken eye.
A new sadness grows on the wild east wind.

Frail waist, a careless girdle knot:
red apricot blooms at branch's tip.
The second moon and spring's still shallow.
I gaze into the distance
and wait in vain for word of you.
Yet should it come...
small solace
compared to your return.

I Love the Hues of Early Spring at West Lake

I love the hues of early spring at West Lake.
Winter snows just melting:
you can see the plum there, blooming, small.
Then, the flicker of the shadows of clouds and
that time's gone.
Now few blossoms remain to light green shade.

Yet you may find in these remaining flowers
one more smile.
So too in the lute song, captive of beauty, embracing. . .
I'm old, these gusts of feeling shouldn't rise.
I depend on you to tip the flowing bowl once more.

Ten Years, and Now Together; a Cup of Wine

Ten years, and now together; a cup of wine.

When old friends meet, they take their ease.

How often anymore have you or I companions in our pleasures?

In this floating life, the joys of song

are easiest to lose.

Duties and travels; who can predict,

when we may meet, again, must part?

Don't be ashamed to be drunk as mud.

Blushing, They Comb Their Dark, Iridescent Hair

Blushing, they comb their dark, iridescent hair,
and when it's done they turn.
With swan's neck lute of thirteen strings
one by one, each spring oriole will sing.

Pretty clouds, flown with the changes,
the dream gone, and where am I?
The quiet court has melted into dusk.
Gust upon gust, rain falls on the plantain.

Butterflies Flown in the Fragrant Grasses

Butterflies flown in fragrant grasses,
flowers down the road.
I raise the cup and sigh; spring's colors, sunset.
Faded flowers fall from the branch.
Now, flown on the stream, gone where?

Before the hall I wander by a tree where autumn locusts sing,
remembering when I warmed the first buds with my breath.
The summer's scarlet lotus, green artemisia pale,
these, now, grow full perfumed,
but can't outlast the vengeful wind:
jade cold white frost; the fall.

So Deep, So Deep the Court, How Deep?

So deep, so deep, the court, how deep?
Willows heaped in countless loose-hung curtains,
fine-tooled tack and saddle, wander, melt away.
Though the tower's high, I cannot see the highway.

A mad wind drives rain across March night.
I close the door against the dusk,
but find no way to hold the spring.
Crying, I'd ask flowers, but flowers cannot speak.
Red petals flutter past an old rope swing.

Lotus Leaves, Field upon Field,
Shine Green upon the Water

Lotus leaves, field upon field, shine green upon the water.

My lonely boat rests moored in flowered shade.

Last night light rain, its hushing, fell.

I could not sleep.

Morning came, and I rose to a wind from the west.

Rains battering, wind's wrench, golden buds all broken.

Only acacia's crested fragrant blooms remain.

Lotus, and a man the same, no lasting satisfactions:

year upon year this bitter fragrance at our hearts.

Ruffed Blue-Green Fields, Red Blossoms

Ruffed blue-green fields, red blossoms,
clear skies fill the eye.
Orioles drift above embroidered mats,
flit up and down together.
On purpled paths and dust gold wagon tracks,
my horse's hooves tread spring land's green.

A sudden spring dream
crowded with my years,
the past so far, so far.
Enough, a hundred kinds of pondering...
Though misting rain fills the tower,
the line of mountains stands unbroken.
Idly a man tries everywhere
to find some crook of rail to lean on.

At P'ing Shan, by the Rail

At P'ing Shan, by the rail,
I lean to sunlit emptiness,
the mountain's colors in the mist
now there, now gone.
I planted willows here by hand...
As you leave, the spring's breeze goes too,
caressing them.

"The Literary Governor" they call me...
one flourish of the brush, ten thousand words –
one draught, a thousand cups.
Such joys are for the young, they say...
Behind this cup
you'll find a wrinkled face.

All Day Long along the Curling Dike

All day long along the curling dike
we sail in painted skiff,
in the misty grass the wind soughs, distance,
the sunlight's on the river –
waters mount blue heaven.
Wind, waves, wrinkle,
flowering mallow festoons the oars.
Beauties flutter beauty as they sing,
and startled ducks fly off in pairs.
Come drain the golden cup...
don't think of the past and grow weary.

At the Lookout, Plum Blossoms Scattered

At the lookout, plum blossoms scattered,
slender willows by the bridge above the stream.
Warm winds from misty grasses stirred your reins,
parting's sorrow rode beside you,
and yet it is not gone,
runs like a spring freshet, always on.

A small, a gentle sorrow,
yet a rush of staining tears.
The tower's high, I won't go near the railing.
Spring Mount's as far as I could see from here:
you've gone beyond there now.

Face Turned to Falling Flowers;
A Breeze, Ripples on the Water

Face turned to falling flowers; a breeze, ripples on the water.
Willows deep in mist again, a snow of catkins flying.
Rain gone, a light chill lingers.
Spring's sorrows mix with wine, and I grow sick and weary.
Wind in the curtain by my pillow surrounds me in green waves.
Blue-green ruff of bedcloths, flower of the lamp,
night after night I stare unstirring:
silent, I rise and lift the screen.
Bright moon just at the pear branch tip:
a pair, apart.

At Huang-hua Monastery

By footlog, crossing the deep torrent,
wearing the dew, I pluck savory ferns.
Woodcutter's songs and the sound of sutras
return together to the pines.
Sunset, cold mountain, sad.
Clouds float, my cloak.

Swallow Falls

Swallows return here
to cold heights to dart through flying waters.
My friends gone, my heart sees them:
a flash of pure brilliance, glistening, long.

Evening, Mounting the Heights at Grassy-Bank

Colors of the wilds
                              mix in the sunlit mist.
In all that vast expanse
                              you can make out just one clouded tree.
Some traveler goes down the mountain road,
still trudging toward the capital.

Sound of the Bell as We Ford the Cold Stream

Sound of the bell as we ford the cold stream,
together searching for cloudy peaks,
then follow the lonely bird on down,
glancing back at the towering grove.
Pure sutras sound, distant, still audible.
Sunset:
the empty mountain's song.

At the Grave of Po Chu-I

We offer fragrant herbs and pour libations,
mourning you here among the pines.
At the stream's mouth we gazed toward the peak:
floating clouds
                    were all we saw.

Stone Tower

Rapids rush and rush again,
wind rages:

> the boat's hard to steer.

I'll never see who's resting at the tower.

Mountains flutter past like swallows.

Evening sun on a distant island: all I can see:

the white terns soar.

Far Off Mountains

Mountain colors, up close, far off,
all day going, as I gaze at the crags.
Different peaks in view from every different place:
I will not know their names.

Returning in the Moonlight to Huang-hua

Joy's in the sound of the spring up the cliff,
evening, late, the mountains quiet.
Pines, in a wash of moonlight,
a thousand peaks, a single hue.

Drifting at I-ch'uan

A spring stream slowly grows in the gorge,
ripples raise and turn the tiny boat.
Birds on the sand turn too:

                                away from me

and fly, to the grove's green tips.

Tree on the Mountainside

The old tree rests on the mountainside,
great trunk long coiled in stone.
In the mountains: cruel frost, sleet.
It's late, and yet no sign of spring.
But down beneath the ledge,
cassia blossoms open, stay the wanderer awhile.

Eight Step Rapids

A jumble of stones writes on the water.
Waves leap, a froth like snow.

Travelers on the stream, morning and evening,
each wrung with worry at the rapid's breadth,
wait till these, like floating clouds, are passed:
a lone boat plays ripples
                            the bright moon.

Lang-yeh Creek

Mountain snows melt,
>   swell the stream.
I cross on a tree felled long ago.
No way to know
>   the distance to the source:
watch it rush
>   from among mountain flowers.

About the Translator

J. P. Seaton is professor of Chinese at the University of North Carolina, Chapel Hill, and has translated selected poems of Tu Fu (*Bright Moon, Perching Bird,* Wesleyan University Press, 1987) and a selection of Taoist drinking songs from the Yuan dynasty (*The Wine of Endless Life,* Ardis Press, 1978). He has also translated Francois Cheng's *L'ecriture poetique chinoise* (*Chinese Poetic Writing,* Indiana University Press, 1982).

The type is Kennerley, designed by F.W. Goudy.

Composition by The Typeworks, in Vancouver, B.C.

Book design by Tree Swenson.

Book manufactured by McNaughton & Gunn.